YOUR KNOWLEDGE HAS

Anke Grundmann

The concept of time in Peter Ackroyd's "Hawksmoor"

GRIN Verlag

Bibliografische Information der Deutschen Nationalbibliothek:

Die Deutsche Bibliothek verzeichnet diese Publikation in der Deutschen National-
bibliografie; detaillierte bibliografische Daten sind im Internet über http://dnb.d-
nb.de/ abrufbar.

Imprint:

Copyright © 2000 GRIN Verlag GmbH
Druck und Bindung: Books on Demand GmbH, Norderstedt Germany
ISBN: 978-3-638-70574-5

This book at GRIN:

http://www.grin.com/en/e-book/38799/the-concept-of-time-in-peter-ackroyd-s-
hawksmoor

Universität Bielefeld
Fakultät für Linguistik und Literaturwissenschaft
Wintersemester 1999/2000
Seminar: Prosa der Postmoderne

The Concept of Time

in

Peter Ackroyd's *Hawksmoor*

Anke Ostermann
9. Semester
Studiengang:
MA Literaturwissenschaft, Anglistik, Geschichtswissenschaft

CONTENTS

„Now, now is the Hour, every Hour, every part of an Hour, every Moment, which in its end does begin again and never ceases to end: a beginning continuing, always ending."

Peter Ackroyd, *Hawksmoor*, 62.

0. Introduction

Usually a novel contains a beginning, a middle and an end. That is what the reader expects from the majority of books. This convention is not only based on the presumption that only by this sequence of beginning, middle and end a reader will find the reading of a novel rewarding but there are also theoretical concepts demanding this structure. Mendilow points out that Aristotle was one of the first to stress the meaning of a general structure in a piece of literature.[1] According to Aristotle

> [e]in Ganzes ist, was Anfang, Mitte und Ende hat. Ein Anfang ist, was selbst nicht mit Notwendigkeit auf etwas anderes folgt, nach dem jedoch natürlicherweise etwas anderes eintritt oder entsteht. Ein Ende ist umgekehrt, was selbst natürlicherweise auf etwas anderes folgt, und zwar notwendigerweise oder in der Regel, während nach ihm nichts anderes mehr eintritt. Eine Mitte ist, was sowohl selbst auf etwas anderes folgt als auch etwas anderes nach sich zieht.[2]

This concept is true for realistic novels but it falls short for most of the postmodern novels.

In this paper I will show how the structure of a linear plot is given up in Peter Ackroyd's novel *Hawksmoor*. The sequence of beginning, middle and end evokes that all events are linked by a chain of causality or as Patricia Drechsel Tobin puts it „[...] events in time come to be perceived as begetting other events within a line of causality [...]."[3] In *Hawksmoor* the chain of causality and the linear concept of time are replaced by a circular concept of time. The events in the novel and in particular the murders cannot be explained by the principle of causality.

In my paper I will analyse the concept of time in Ackroyd's novel. As a first step I will point out the relation of the novel to the historical figure Nicholas Hawksmoor and summarise briefly the two plots so that on this basis the analogies and recurrences in each plot can be better understood. Chapter 3 deals with the conception of characters because it is the repetition of characteristics, biographies and attitudes of the characters

---

[1] Cf. A.A. Mendilow, *Time And The Novel* (New York: Humanities Press, 1972) 45.
[2] Aristoteles, *Poetik*, trans. and ed. Manfred Fuhrmann (Stuttgart: Reclam, 1996) 25.
[3] Patricia Drechsel Tobin, *Time And The Novel. The Genealogical Imperative* (Princeton: Princeton University Press, 1978) 7.

that illustrate best the linear concept of time. The character that is associated the most with this concept of time is the protagonist of the eighteenth-century plot Nicholas Dyer. Therefore, I choose this figure for a detailed analysis in chapter 4. Apart from the motif of time, the dualism of rationality and irrationality plays an important role in the novel. Since the aim of this paper is to examine how the motif „time" is represented the contrast between the two opposing ideologies will be analysed only in so far how it illustrates that progress as a symbol of the concept of linear time is denied just as the singularity of everyday events.

For this reason, a full study of the contrast between the two world pictures represented by Christopher Wren as the adherent of Enlightenment and Dyer who believes in Satanism and the power of symbols is impossible. Moreover, I have to refrain from a detailed analysis of the twentieth-century plot as a detective novel. Although murders and the investigations of a detective are typical elements of this genre this study will concentrate on the functions these elements have in connection with the concept of continuity and circular time.[4]

1. The Title *Hawksmoor*

The title of Peter Ackroyd's novel refers to Nicholas Hawksmoor, an English architect who was born 1661 and died in 1736. He was a pupil of Sir Christopher Wren and in 1711 he became a member of the commission that was responsible for the construction of new churches in London.[5] Although the historical figure does not appear in the text the title „gives the 'real' Hawksmoor a presence in the novel by his very absence from it".[6] The two fictitious protagonists in the novel are linked to this real character in different ways. The architect Nicholas Dyer shares the profession with him, whereas

---

[4] For *Hawksmoor* as a form of the detective novel see Alison Lee, *Realism and Power. Postmodern British Fiction* (London: Routledge, 1990) 69 and Susanne Spekat, „Postmoderne Gattungshybriden: Peter Ackroyd's *Hawksmoor* als generische Kombination aus *historical novel, gothic novel* und *detective novel*," *Literatur in Wissenschaft und Unterricht* 30 (1997): 194-197.
[5] Cf. „Hawksmoor, Nicholas," *Encyclopædia Britannica*, Chicago: Benton, 1967 ed.
[6] Lee, *Realism and Power*, 84.

Detective Chief Superintendent Nicholas Hawksmoor bares the same name as the historical figure.[7]

By this, not only do Ackroyd's two characters possess fragments of a real person's identity, but they are also linked with each other. Only in combining aspects of two identities, Dyer's profession and Hawksmoor's full name the relation of the two characters to the real Nicholas Hawksmoor becomes clear. In creating characters who are connected by such a strong relation the author anticipates the end of the novel that can be read as the fusion of two identities beyond the bounds of time which will be discussed in chapter 3.

2. The Plots

The novel which is divided into twelve chapters (chapters 1 to 5 constituting part one and chapters 6 to 12 constituting part two) contains two plots. The odd-numbered chapters are set in the eighteenth century and are written in an eighteenth-century English, whereas the setting of the even-numbered chapters is the twentieth century, presumably the 1980s. The chapters are presented in an alternate structure. Each of the two plots has its own starting point which is divided by temporal distance of approximately 270 years but they share a common end. In both plots the protagonists enter the church of Little St Hugh in order to fuse to one identity at the end of the novel.

2.1 Plot A

The protagonist of the eighteenth-century plot or plot A as I will call it in my paper, is Nicholas Dyer, „Assistant Surveyour at Her Majesty's Office of Works".[8] This

---

[7] Cf. Brad Leithauser, „Thrown Voices," *New Yorker* 8 February 1988: 100.
[8] Peter Ackroyd, *Hawksmoor* (London: Penguin, 1993) 10.

character is modelled on the real Hawksmoor although Dyer is born seven years earlier than Hawksmoor, i.e. in 1654 and dies in 1715. Like the famous architect he is commissioned to build seven new churches in London because many buildings were destroyed by a fire in 1666. In detail, the churches who are erected are Christ Church in Spitalfields, St Anne's in Limehouse, St George's-in-the-East in Wapping, St Mary Woolnoth in Lombard Street, St George's in Bloomsbury, St Alfege's in Greenwich and Little St Hugh in Black Step Lane. All these churches were built by the historical Nicholas Hawksmoor except for the last church. Little St Hugh is an invention of Ackroyd situated in a fictitious area of London.

When Dyer was a child his parents died of the plague. He became a street urchin and was introduced by the Satanist Mirabilis to occultism and the rules of the Satanic cult. After becoming a Satanist himself, Dyer consecrates each of his new churches with a human sacrifice. The blood of the victim who is either killed by Dyer himself or by a helper has to be spilled on the grounds of the church and the corpse is buried in the foundations. According to the rules of the Satanic cult all victims have to be virgin: [...] in our Eucharist the Bread must be mingled with the Blood of an Infant.'[9] Therefore, most victims are boys or childlike men.

2.2 Plot B

The main character of plot B is Superintendent Nicholas Hawksmoor who is assigned to solve a series of murders all committed in the area of churches built by Dyer. Although Hawksmoor is used to solve a crime with the help of rationality and scientific methods he realises the impossibility of finding the murderer because conventional methods as the determination of the time of the incident and the examination of the witnesses lead nowhere. During the investigations he becomes more and more psychotic not least because of the fact that he, as Luc Herman puts it „[...] must realize [...] that this case

---

[9] Ibid., 20.

transcends the laws of cause and effect."[10] It is only at the end of the novel that he realises the pattern of the killings and that all victims were murdered in the vicinity of churches built by Dyer.

3. The Conception of Characters

3.1 The Victims

Ackroyd establishes a relation between the two plots in giving identical or nearly identical names to the persons killed in the eighteenth-century plot and the victims of the twentieth-century plot. The persons Dyer sacrifices during the construction of his churches are Thomas Hill, a mason's son, the tramp Ned, a boy called Dan, Yorick Hayes, Dyer's colleague and Thomas Robinson. The victim killed in the church of Greenwich is not mentioned by name. The corpses found in the present are Thomas Hill, the son of a widow, the vagrant Edward Robinson, called Ned, Dan Dee and Matthew Hayes. The name of the fifth and sixth victim are not stated, but presumably the person found at St George's in Bloomsbury is called Thomas Robinson like Dyer's fifth victim.

Not only bare the victims the same names but they also have similar biographies. This identity of characteristics and life can be seen most clearly in the case of the second victim Edward (Ned) Robinson. Both had been a printer in Bristol but due to mental problems gave up their profession and became a tramp.

This repetition of names and characteristics has the effect that the reader after reading a chapter set in the eighteenth century knows who will be killed in the subsequent twentieth-century chapter. In *Hawksmoor* the concept of individuality is given up. There are no individual characters but only certain characteristics recurring in the course of time.

Die Wiederholung von Eigenschaften und Merkmalen in der Figurencharakterisierung der

---

[10] Luc Herman, „The Relevance of History: *Der Zauberbaum* (1985) by Peter Sloterdijk and *Hawksmoor* (1985) by Peter Ackroyd," *History and Post-war Writing*, ed. Theo D'haen and Hans Bertens (Amsterdam: Rodopi, 1990): 117.

> Protagonisten weist auf eine anti-realistische Figurenkonzeption hin, für die Individualität kein gültiges Persönlichkeitsmodell mehr bildet. Die Figuren erscheinen nicht länger als selbstbestimmte Subjekte, die ihr Schicksal lenken, sondern vielmehr als Repräsentanten von überzeitlichen menschlichen Erfahrungen von Entfremdung vom Selbst und von anderen, von Einsamkeit, Hoffnungslosigkeit und Verzweiflung.[11]

Since the persons killed by Dyer and the murders investigated by Hawksmoor share the name and other characteristics each murder happens twice: Dyer's murders are repeated in the twentieth century and by this each victim dies twice. The consequence is a continual cycle of life and death. Although Dyer's Satanic rituals have never been discovered and nobody is aware of that the churches are consecrated by their architect to Satan instead of God some victims of plot B have visions of what happened to their namesake in the eighteenth century. Thomas Hill experiences in a vision the last moments in the life of the mason's son before he dies: „And then he was climbing towards them, climbing the tower until the clouds hid him, climbing the tower as a voice called out, *Go on! Go on!*"[12] This fusion of time levels is even more emphasised when a tourist standing in front of Christ Church in Spitalfields (the church where in plot A Thomas Hill was killed) thinks that he has seen something falling from the tower: „What was that falling there?"[13] Occurrences of the past intermingle with the present. In passages like this both plots are not separated by a temporal distance but happen simultaneously.

Moreover, persons belonging to the present seem to have unconsciously memories of the lives of their dead namesakes. When the tramp Ned decides to leave his apartment for ever in order to live on the streets he feels this step to be a familiar and predetermined one: „[...] when he walked into Severndale Park he felt the breeze bringing back memories of a much earlier life, and he was at peace."[14] His encounter with a person dressed in a „dark coat"[15] is analogous to the encounter of the tramp with Dyer in the eighteenth century. In plot A the situation of the murder is narrated from Dyer's perspective whereas in plot B the point of view changes to the victim Ned. Due

---

[11] Spekat, „Postmoderne Gattungshybriden," 190.
[12] Ackroyd, *Hawksmoor*, 30.
[13] Ibid., 26.
[14] Ibid., 75.
[15] Ibid., 68.

to a phonetic identity of the words spoken by Dyer, the old-fashioned expression „Ay me"[16] and the words „I" and „me" Ned who is not accustomed to the language of the early eighteenth century does not recognise the meaning of the words spoken by his murderer.

3.2 Dyer and Hawksmoor

As I have mentioned before the most obvious relation between Dyer and Hawksmoor is the title of the novel. From the title *Hawksmoor* the reader could assume that the novel is a biography about the historical Nicholas Hawksmoor. The author plays with the expectations of the reader in giving a different name, Dyer, to the character that is meant as a counterpart to the real Hawksmoor but at the same time creating a fictitious character of the present named Hawksmoor. Only the synthesis of the two protagonists represents what can be expected from the title *Hawksmoor*.

At first glance, the role allocation is clear. In plot A Dyer is the murderer, whereas in plot B Hawksmoor is the detective searching for the culprit. With the help of this classification based on moral values, Dyer being the „bad" and Hawksmoor the „good", the two characters are clearly distinguished at the beginning. The only link between them is the corpses. As Brenda Maddox says: „Dyer' corpses are Hawksmoor' s corpses. One makes them, the other discovers them [...]."[17]

In the course of the novel the distinction starts to become blurred. The more Hawksmoor tries to solve the crimes the more he adopts Dyer's behaviour and thoughts. After the third victim had been discovered at St George's-in-the-East in Wapping Hawksmoor walks from the scene of the crime to the places where Dyer's first two victims were killed, St Anne' s Limehouse and Christ Church in Spitalfields. He follows Dyer's way backwards both in the sense of time and space. Regarding space, he walks from the scene of the crime of the third murder back to the scenes of the crime of the second and first murder. In addition to this, he also moves backward in time since

---

[16] Ibid., 66.
[17] Brenda Maddox, „ Murder most holy," *The Listener* 5 December 1985: 30.

he follows Dyer's stations where he committed his crimes. The detective sees his job as „hurry[ing] the murderer along the course which he had already laid for himself".[18] That is exactly what he is doing during his walk. At the end of his walk he reaches Christ Church, the place where in both plots the first victim was killed. The starting point of Dyer's „criminal career" becomes the end of Hawksmoor's way. This identity of ways can be seen as a first sign of fusion of the two characters.

Apart from this, there are other analogies between Dyer and Hawksmoor. Both become fragmented personalities. In the case of Dyer the constant fear of being discovered as a Satanist and murderer leads to such an enormous mental pressure that he cannot perceive himself as a complete entity any more: „Who is that worshipful Lump of Clay, that Thing which lolls by the Stove in an Elbow-chair? That Thing is me, [...]".[19] The effect the investigation has on Hawksmoor is similar. His mind and his body cease to be a unity:

> [...] [D]uring the course of the afternoon he tried to look at himself as if he were a stranger, so that he might be able to predict his next step. Time passes, and he looks down at his own hands and wonders if he would recognise them if they lay severed upon a table.[20]

Not only does he question the meaning of his own personality, but also the language loses its meaning and rationality for him. In his view, the chain of causality of the spoken words seems to be lacking . Words become meaningless fragments.

> 'Well if you feel up to it,' one young man was saying, 'You could do that. This is true. This is true.' And then his companion answered, 'But it was raining'. Hawksmoor watched them standing together and wondered if there was any connection between the two remarks: he considered the matter carefully as the men moved a few inches backward and forward as they talked, and concluded that there was none. He listened again and he heard the phrases, 'I fell asleep', 'I dreamed' and 'I woke up' - and he repeated to himself the words, 'asleep', 'dreamed' and 'woke' to see if their shape or sound accounted for their position in the sequence which the two men were unfolding. And he saw no reason for them; and he saw no reason for the words he himself used, [...].[21]

For Hawksmoor the environment is not a coherent unity any more but there are only fragments which have no link to each other. Both Dyer and Hawksmoor seem to consider themselves not as a part of their current present but somehow are extracted

---

[18] Ackroyd, *Hawksmoor*, 116.
[19] Ibid., 131.
[20] Ibid., 202.

9

from the context they live in.[22] A further common feature of Dyer and Hawksmoor indicating that they are supernaturally linked to the past and future is their ability so see and feel what the victims of a murderer felt before they were killed.[23]

The fusion of the two characters becomes even more explicit when Hawksmoor compares his profession to the profession of an architect: „Hawksmoor liked to measure these discrete phases, which he considered as an architect might consider the plan of a building [...]."[24] Both Dyer and Hawksmoor seem to be obsessed with trying to structure their environment. While Dyer wants to create new buildings after the city of London had been destroyed by the Great Fire and the plague, Hawksmoor's way of coping with death is to look at it scientifically.

The difference between Dyer and Hawksmoor is their attitude to reason and sciences. Whereas Dyer does not believe in rationalism, Hawksmoor at the beginning relies on rational methods and so echoes the position of Sir Christopher Wren, Dyer's mentor. The detective thinks that the crime can be solved with the help of modern methods of investigation:

> [...] [H]e liked to consider himself as a scientist, or even as a scholar, since it was from close observation and rational deduction that he came to a proper understanding of each case; he prided himself on his acquaintance with chemistry, anatomy and even mathematics since it was these disciplines which helped him to resolve situations at which others trembled. For he knew that even during extreme events the laws of cause and effect still operated; [...].[25]

Since the time of the incident cannot be determined Hawksmoor recognises that rational methods fall short. Contrary to his conviction at the beginning he starts to understand that the laws of cause and effect are not valid in this case. Like Dyer he gives up the linear concept time trying to trace the murder backwards, „running the time slowly in the opposite direction".[26] In the course of the investigations Hawksmoor comes to the conclusion that there is no such thing as the linear sequence of past, present and future. At Greenwich he tries to find the zero meridian and cannot find it. His inability to find the

---

21 Ibid., 117.
22 Cf. ibid., 152 and 203.
23 Cf. ibid., 97-98 and 114.
24 Ibid., 113.
25 Ibid., 152-153.
26 Ibid., 157.

place that determines the time zones shows that there is no time or that time is an arbitrary concept at least.[27]

> At such times the future became so clear that it was as if he were remembering it, remembering it in place of the past which he could no longer describe. But there was in any case no future and no past, only the unspeakable misery of his own self.[28]

Before these analogies of behaviour and characteristics culminate in the fusion of Dyer and Hawksmoor at the end of the novel, they encounter each other. In contrast to a realistic novel dealing with the conventional linear concept of time the encounter of two persons living in different levels of time is possible in Ackroyd's novel. According to Michail Bachtin two conditions are necessary so that an encounter takes place in a literary text. Both persons have to be at the same place at the same time. If one condition is not fulfilled the motif „encounter" changes from positive (the encounter did happen) to negative (the encounter did not happen) because either one of the two was at the wrong time at the right place or vice versa.[29] These conditions are not valid for postmodern texts like *Hawksmoor*. Here only one condition, being at the same place, is fulfilled. The fulfilment of the second condition (the same time) is strictly speaking impossible because Dyer and Hawksmoor live in different centuries. In spite of this the two characters meet because the linear concept of time is given up.

Bachtin stresses the meaning of the motif „encounter" as a symbol for the intersection of different biographies when he says that

> [a]uf dem Wege [...] überschneiden sich in einem einzigen zeitlichen und räumlichen Punkt die zeitlichen und räumlichen Wege der verschiedenartigsten Menschen, der Vetreter aller Schichten und Stände, aller Glaubensbekenntnisse, Nationalitäten und Altersstufen. Hier kann es zufällig zu Begegnungen zwischen denjenigen kommen, die normalerweise durch die soziale Hierarchie und durch räumliche Entfernungen voneinander getrennt sind, hier können alle möglichen Kontraste entstehen, können verschiedene Schicksale zusammenstoßen und sich miteinander verflechten.[30]

With regard to Ackroyd's novel one could add that here the encounter of the two protagonists does not only bridge spatial or social distances but also the distance of two

---

[27] Ibid., 188-189.
[28] Ibid., 199.
[29] Cf. Michail Bachtin, *Formen der Zeit im Roman. Untersuchungen zur historischen Poetik*, trans. Michael Dewey, ed. Edward Kowalski and Michael Wegner (Frankfurt am Main: Fischer, 1989) 22.
[30] Ibid., 192.

11

centuries. Time is not a barrier any longer. Dyer sees Hawksmoor in his visions,[31] whereas Hawksmoor meets Dyer near Christ Church, who in plot B is called „the Architect".[32] Parallel to having visions of what can be called their counterpart both Dyer and Hawksmoor become unable to recognise their own reflection. The situations in which they look at themselves are almost identical:

> [...] by Hogg Lane I [i.e. Dyer] met with my own Apparition - with Habit, Wigg, and everything as in a Looking-glass. Do I know you? I call'd out, much to the Bewilderment of those who passed by, but the Thing did not answer me and walked quickly away.[33]

> [...] as he passed the Red Gates, he noticed his own reflection in the frosted window, beneath a sign for Beers and Spirits. The reflection turned to stare at him before walking on: Hawksmoor passed his hands across his face and then called out, 'Do I know you?' and several passers-by stopped in astonishment as he ran out into the road crying. 'Do I? Do ?'[34]

The boundaries between the own identity, the reflection and visions become indistinguishable so that the characters „grow fragmentary - become beings whose missing portions quest through another era."[35]

Like the victims Dyer and Hawksmoor lose their individuality and fuse to one character in the church of Little St Hugh. The difference between the murderer Dyer and the detective Hawksmoor on the one hand and the difference between the past, i.e. the eighteenth century and the present, .i.e. the twentieth-century on the other hand is cancelled. This fusion has its counterpart on the level of the formal aspects. Whereas plot A is told by Dyer himself in the first person, the chapters of plot B dealing with Hawksmoor's investigations are written in the third person. The last sentences of the novel when Dyer and Hawksmoor speak „with one voice"[36] the author uses the first-person narration so that the „I" refers to both characters.[37] Dyer and Hawksmoor have fused to one single person.

---

11 Cf. Ackroyd, *Hawksmoor*, 205 and 206.
11 Cf. ibid., 196.
11 Ibid., 206.
11 Ibid., 211.
11 Leithauser, „Thrown Voices," 102.
11 Ackroyd, *Hawksmoor*, 217.
11 Cf. Annegret Maack, „Der Roman als 'Echokammer': Peter Ackroyds Erzählstrategien," *Tales and „their telling difference". Zur Theorie und Geschichte der Narrativik*. Festschrift für Franz K. Stanzel, ed. Herbert Foltinek et al. (Heidelberg: Winter, 1993): 333.

4. Dyer's Concept of Time

Names, characteristics and situations always recur in the novel. Dyer himself believes strongly in this circular concept of time. The idea that people who were killed in the past can be reborn only to suffer the same death in the present is anticipated by him when he compares the cycle of life of human beings to the cycle of nature:

> [...] my Church will take great Profit from it: this Mirabilis once describ'd to me, *viz* a Corn when it dies and rots in the Ground, it springs again and lives, so, *said he*, when there are many Persons dead, only being buryed and laid in the Earth, there is an Assembling of Powers.[38]

By building his church where the victims of the plague were buried the place is supposed to become so powerful that the dead will rise again. Dyer denies the idea of the finality of death and the linear concept of time. In doing so he follows the rules of his Satanic cult. Since the idea of a linear time is characteristic for Western cultures and the Christian religion in particular[39] Dyer as an adherent of occultism and black magic has to reject this concept of time. In his opinion not only will the dead return but every event is part of an eternal cycle. The singularity of the moment does not exist:

> Truly Time is a vast Denful of Horrour, round about which a Serpent winds and in the winding bites itself by the Tail. Now, now is the Hour, every Hour, every part of an Hour, every Moment, which in its end does begin again and never ceases to end: a beginning continuing, always ending.[40]

Not only is this concept of time described explicitly by Dyer but it is also illustrated by the fusion of events of the present and memories of the past. Several times Dyer interrupts his narration in order to shift back to events in his childhood.

> We must make Haste, *I call'd* taking Pen and Inke, for the Church must be compleat

---

Maack points out that in view of this fusion it is not clear who the narrator of the chapters set in the eighteenth century is. Since Hawksmoor speaks in the first person at the end he might also be the narrator of plot A.

[38] Ackroyd, *Hawksmoor*, 23.
[39] Cf. Drechsel Tobin, *Time And The Novel*, 12-14.
[40] Ackroyd, *Hawksmoor*, 62.

withinne the Year. *And the yeares turn so fast, adds Walter,* and now he is vanish'd and I am gone back to the time of the Distemper when I went abroad among so many walking Carcasses sweating Poison.[41]

Dyer does not narrate his life in a linear order but all levels of time are presented parallel to the reader.

Moreover, there are also passages that are narrated in the present tense. By this, past and future are faded out and the emphasis in on the present moment.

> Now I hear him scratching a Coppy of my Draught, and as I leave the Sphere of Memory I hear the Noises of the World in which I am like to Drown: a Door creaks upon its Hinge, a Crow calls, a Voice is raised and I am no thing againe, [...].[42]

According to Annegret Maack this use of tenses aims at the „Vergegenwärtigung des Erzählten".[43] The chronological order of the past, present and future is cancelled. The consequences are twofold. On the one hand the present becomes the most important temporal element as it can be seen in the passage just quoted. On the other hand all time levels exist simultaneously. According to Maack this concept of time reflects the postmodern idea of intertextuality. Since neither the time levels of the eighteenth century and the twentieth century nor the chapters dealing with these time levels are separated (by the means of an alternate arrangement) a simultaneity of events and texts arise or, as Maack puts it, a simultaneous „Verfügbarkeit der Prätexte"[44] is created.

A symbol of this circular concept of time is the churches built by Dyer. For him they are the constants in the eternal cycle of life and death. Since the killings in both plots happen near the churches they form the relation between the past and the present. The meaning of the churches as symbols of constancy and eternity is also perceived by Hawksmoor:

> [...] [F]or him it was only now, after this death, that it [the church] emerged with the clarity and definition which it must have possessed for those who looked upon it when it was first built. Hawksmoor had often noticed how, in the moments when he first came upon a corpse, all the objects around it wavered for an instant and became unreal - the trees which rose

---

[41] Ibid., 18.
[42] Ibid., 22.
[43] Maack, „Der Roman als 'Echokammer'," 334.
Maack also points out that the use of the present tense indicates a lesser degree of fictionality than the past tense. In plot A both past and present tense are used whereas in plot B the author only uses the past tense in order to emphasise the fictional character of the narration.
[44] Ibid.

above a body hidden in woodland, the movement of the river which had washed a body onto its banks, the cars or hedges in a suburban street where a murderer had left a victim, all of these things seemed at such times to be suddenly drained of meaning like an hallucination. But this church has grown larger and more distinct in the face of death.[45]

Eventually Dyer fuses with his last church Little St Hugh in Black Step Lane. He himself becomes immortal by becoming part of the church. His existence is absorbed by the building but only Hawksmoor two centuries later is able to see this fusion of architect and building that is symbolised by a „circular window above the porch"[46] shaped like an eye.

5. Rationality vs. Irrationality

Both plots are set at a time when radical social and cultural changes happen. Especially in plot A the end of the medieval world picture and the beginning of rationalism and Enlightenment are a central theme, but also in the twentieth-century plot the beginning of the computer generation characterises the atmosphere of the novel. The motif „computer" as the symbol for universal knowledge is omnipresent.[47] Dyer is the representative of an out-dated ideology based on occultism and admiration of the Ancients. For him logic and ratiocination are only despicable concepts and unsuitable to replace the belief in the Ancients: „And so while others were mouthing such fantasticall and perishable Trash, I kept to my studdy of the antient Architects, for the greatness of the Antients is infinitely superior to the Moderns."[48] His opponents are his colleague Sir John Vanbrugghe (sic), Priddon and in particular Sir Christopher Wren, who as a member of the Royal Society represents the new sciences by saying:

> [...] we have learned that the Experimentall Philosophy is an Instrument for Mankind's domination of Darknesse and Superstition [...] and that through the Sciences of Mechanicks, Opticks, Hydrostaticks, Pneumaticks as well as Chymistry, Anatomy and the Mathematicall Arts we have begun to understand the works of Nature [...].[49]

---

[45] Ackroyd, *Hawksmoor*, 155-156.
[46] Ibid., 216.
[47] Cf. ibid., 123 and 160.
[48] Ibid., 56.
[49] Ibid., 140.

He does not share Dyer's view that „[t]he things of the Earth must be understood by the sentient Faculties, not by the Understanding"[50] but is of the opinion that new scientific methods mark the beginning of a new era.

> Of all nations we were most us'd to order our Affairs by Omens and Praedictions, until we reached this Enlightened Age: for it is now the fittest season for Experiments to arise, to teach us the New Science which springs from Observation and Demonstration and Reason and Method, to shake off the Shaddowes and to scatter the Mists which fill the Minds of Men with a vain Consternation.[51]

Whereas rationalism and Enlightenment have not yet completely replaced the medieval world picture in plot A, in the twentieth century the use of scientific methods during the investigations has become normal. It is Hawksmoor himself who believes that „[m]urders aren't unsolveable"[52] because with the help of rational methods the culprit will be identified. In the course of his investigations he realises that he is wrong. In each case the time of the incident cannot be determined. Either the examinations of the autopsy lead to contradictory conclusions or time seems to be a factor that is mysteriously missing. According to one of the witnesses who found the fourth victim the murders are not part of any concept of time but exist independently because „[t]here was no time."[53] Moreover both the witnesses of the murders committed by Dyer and the twentieth-century murders all have „a confuse'd sense of Time"[54] or give contradictory testimonies. The murders are presented as something that blurs and distorts the factor time. Since they go beyond the scope of time investigations based on a linear concept of time fall short. Although it is only at the end of the novel that Hawksmoor realises that the crimes have a stronger connection to the past than he first assumed he is aware of the fact that the murders are untimely.

> And it was important for him, also, to master his subject so thoroughly that he knew the seasons and the rules of death: stabbings and strangulations were popular in the late eighteenth century, for example, slashed throats and clubbings in the early nineteenth, poison and mutilation in the latter part of the last century. This was one reason why the recent cases of strangling, culminating in the third corpse at Wapping, seemed to him to be quite unusual - to be taking place at the wrong time.[55]

---

[50] Ibid., 144.
[51] Ibid., 145.
[52] Ibid., 126.
[53] Ibid. 157.
[54] Ibid., 172.
[55] Ibid., 117.

All this and the fact that no clues of the murderer can be found convince Hawksmoor that the case cannot be solved by ratiocination because the murders are inexplicable by a chain of causality:

> The event of the boy's death was not simple because it was not unique and if he traced it backwards, running the time slowly in the opposite direction (but did it have a direction?), it became no clearer. The chain of causality might extend as far back as the boy's birth, in a particular place and on a particular date, or even further into the darkness beyond that.[56]

The consequences are twofold: not only does he adopt Dyer's cyclic concept of time, he also starts to believe in irrationality. By realising that Dyer is the reason for the murders he begins to understand that past and present form a unity which he himself is part of or as Alison Lee puts it „[...] he realizes that the structure he has been looking for has an archi-*textual* symmetry which is completed by his own death at the end of the novel.‟[57]

The conviction of the culprit at the end of the novel is characteristic for the detective novel. Although Ackroyd's twentieth-century protagonist so-to-speak solves the crime by identifying Dyer as the murderer the dénouement does not live up to the expectations one would have reading a „normal‟ detective novel since the murders themselves remain mysterious. The conviction of the murderer does not clarify the preceding events but calls rationality into question so that Hawksmoor when discovering

> [...] that all murders are committed in or close by churches of one and the same architect, [...] does *not* regard this as the rational solution that he sought at first, but rather as the confirmation of the idea (rejected by his colleagues) that intellect would fall short in this particular case.[58]

Supernatural phenomena play an important part in Ackroyd's novel. When they occur they always indicate a fusion of time levels. Events of the past and the present normally following each other in a linear concept of time are described simultaneously or in the „wrong‟ temporal order. Hawksmoor's father, for example talks about a letter

---

[56] Ibid., 157.
[57] Lee, *Realism and Power*, 68.
[58] Herman, „The Relevance of History,‟ 117.

Dyer's assistant Walter Pyne wrote of which he can know nothing.[59] Another example for the blurring of the frontier between past and present is the visions of some of the characters in which events of the future are anticipated. In plot A the investigations of Hawksmoor are foreseen when a lunatic warns Dyer: „I'll tell you somewhat, one Hawksmoor will this day terribly shake you!"[60] In a linear concept of time all these events appear to be supernatural because they subvert the principle of singularity. They can only be explained by a circular concept of time in which everything recurs and exists simultaneously.

In passages like this the author illustrates the concept of postmodernism that all levels of time coexist.[61] This assumption allows all events to exist in a time continuum that is not structured by a temporal sequence.

With regard to the ideologies represented in the novel *Hawksmoor* is characterised by a cyclic structure. At the beginning the irrational world picture based on medieval occultism and superstition represented by Dyer prevails. Rationalism and Enlightenment are its opposing currents which have become the dominant ideology in the twentieth-century. The representative of rationality is Hawksmoor. His failure to solve the crimes with the help of rational and scientific methods marks the regression from rationality to irrationality. There seems to be no progress but only the everlasting antagonism of different concepts of ideas.

Some critics interpret the fusion of Dyer and Hawksmoor as the reconciliation of the diametrical concepts of rationality and irrationality.[62] In my opinion this interpretation is problematic, not only because, as Susanne Spekat says,

> [...] alle Figuren, die das mystisch-irrationale Weltbild verinnerlicht haben, infolge der Nichtanschließbarkeit ihres individuellen Wirklichkeitsmodells an die soziale Kommunikation, die vom rationalen Weltbild beherrscht wird, ihre Handlungsfähigkeit verlieren[63]

---

[59] Cf. Ackroyd, *Hawksmoor*, 121.
[60] Ibid., 100.
[61] Cf. Maack, „Der Roman als 'Echokammer'," 334-335.
[62] Cf. Brian Finney, „Peter Ackroyd, Postmodernist Play and *Chatterton*," *Twentieth Century Literature* 38 (1992): 247 and Susana Jaén Onega, quoted in: Spekat, „Postmoderne Gattungshybriden," 198-199.
[63] Spekat, „Postmoderne Gattungshybriden," 199.

but also because the conflict between rationality and irrationality which is exemplary demonstrated in the figure of Hawksmoor is ultimately settled in favour of irrationality. Hawksmoor's attempts to solve the crimes by ratiocination are clearly defeated by the mystic character of the killings. The fusion of the two protagonists means that the identity of the rational detective is absorbed by the representative of irrationality. Hawksmoor himself carries on Dyer's tradition of sacrificial killings by becoming the seventh victim.

6. Summary

The analysis of the novel shows that the concept of time is a cyclic one instead of a linear one which can be found in most novels and especially in realistic novels. In accordance to the postmodern tradition of questioning the singularity and general validity of events the author uses the recurrence of characters and events in order to illustrate his concept of time based on repetition. With regard to the characters one can summarise that the figures are no individuals but they are only types whose characteristics are repeated throughout the novel. In the beginning the two protagonists Dyer and Hawksmoor constitute an exception since they represent opposing scientific concepts but in the course of the novel Hawksmoor adopts more and more the behaviour and attitudes of his eighteenth-century counterpart so that they fuse to one character.

The recurrence of events is most clearly symbolised by the repetition of the murders, statements, behaviour and gestures. Almost every element of the eighteenth-century plot is repeated either completely identical or slightly modified in the present. London and particularly Dyer's churches are the constants that constitute the setting in which all these repetitions are embedded.

Closely linked to the use of repetitions is the question about the origin of things. The impossibility to find a final answer to this question is demonstrated by the failure to convict the murderer. Dyer in not the origin of the murders because he himself imitates the antiquity and follows the traditions of the Satanic cult which has its roots in the rituals of the Druids of pre-Christian times. The constant reference to former eras evokes a simultaneity of time levels. The alternate arrangement of the chapters set in the past and in the present stresses the concept of simultaneity. Neither are past and present distinguishable nor does one era dominate over the other. Since the laws of cause and effect are not valid the existence of a chain of causality is denied. Time is not a linear concept but a continuum without a beginning and an end.

7. Works Cited

Ackroyd, Peter. *Hawksmoor*. London: Penguin, 1993.

Aristoteles. *Poetik*. Trans. and ed. Manfred Fuhrmann. Stuttgart: Reclam, 1996.

Bachtin, Michail M. *Formen der Zeit im Roman. Untersuchungen zur historischen Poetik*. Trans. Michael Dewey. Ed. Edward Kowalski and Michael Wegner. Frankfurt am Main: Fischer, 1989.

Drechsel Tobin, Patricia. *Time And The Novel. The Genealogical Imperative*. Princeton: Princeton University Press, 1978.

Finney, Brian. „Peter Ackroyd, Postmodernist Play and *Chatterton*." *Twentieth Century Literature* 38 (1992). 240-261.

„Hawksmoor, Nicholas." Encyclopædia Britannica. Chicago: Benton, 1967 ed.

Herman, Luc. „The Relevance of History: *Der Zauberbaum* (1985) by Peter Sloterdijk and *Hawksmoor* (1985) by Peter Ackroyd." *History and Post-war Writing*. Ed. Theo D'haen and Hans Bertens. Amsterdam: Rodopi, 1990. 107-124.

Lee, Alison. *Realism and Power. Postmodern British Fiction*. London: Routledge, 1990.

Leithauser, Brad. „Thrown Voices." *New Yorker* (8 February 1988). 99-102.

Maack, Annegret. „Der Roman als 'Echokammer': Peter Ackroyds Erzählstrategien." *Tales and „their telling difference". Zur Theorie und*

Geschichte der Narrativik. Festschrift für Franz K. Stanzel. Ed. Herbert Foltinek et al. Heidelberg: Winter, 1993. 319-335.

Maddox, Brenda. „Murder most holy." *The Listener* (5 December 1985). 30.

Mendilow, A.A. *Time And The Novel*. New York: Humanities Press, 1972.

Spekat, Susanne. „Postmoderne Gattungshybriden: Peter Ackroyds *Hawksmoor* als generische Kombination aus *historical novel*, *gothic novel* und *detective novel*." *Literatur in Wissenschaft und Unterricht* 30 (1997). 183-199.